Amazing Inventions

# Inventing Vaccines

by Matt Lilley

# www.focusreaders.com

Focus Readers is distributed by North Star Editions:
sales@northstareditions.com | 888-417-0195

Produced for Focus Readers by Red Line Editorial.

Photographs ©: Shutterstock Images, cover, 1, 4, 8, 11, 14, 17, 19, 25, 26, 29; iStockphoto, 6, 21, 22; Massoud Hossaini/AP Images, 13

**Library of Congress Cataloging-in-Publication Data**
Names: Lilley, Matt, author.
Title: Inventing vaccines / by Matt Lilley.
Description: Lake Elmo, MN : Focus Readers, [2022] | Series: Amazing inventions | Includes index. | Audience: Grades 2-3
Identifiers: LCCN 2021042109 (print) | LCCN 2021042110 (ebook) | ISBN 9781637390504 (hardcover) | ISBN 9781637391044 (paperback) | ISBN 9781637391587 (ebook) | ISBN 9781637392096 (pdf)
Subjects: LCSH: Vaccines--Juvenile literature. | Vaccines--Research--Juvenile literature. | Vaccines-History--Juvenile literature.
Classification: LCC QR189 .L55 2022 (print) | LCC QR189 (ebook) | DDC 615.3/72--dc23
LC record available at https://lccn.loc.gov/2021042109
LC ebook record available at https://lccn.loc.gov/2021042110

Printed in the United States of America
Mankato, MN
012022

# About the Author

Matt Lilley is the author of more than a dozen books for children. His favorite topics to write about are health, science, technology, biographies, and nature (especially birds and sea creatures). He lives in Minnesota with his family.

# Table of Contents

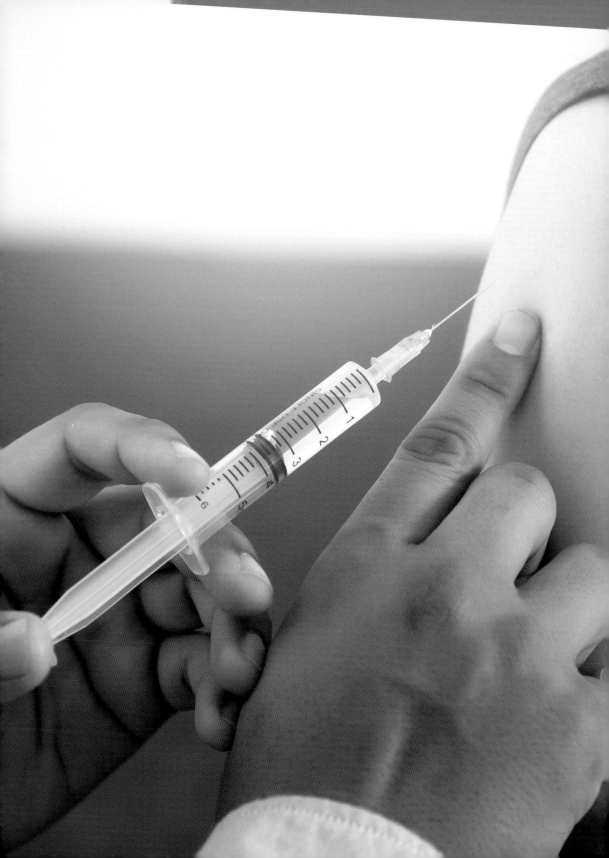

# Chapter 1

# The Flu Shot

It was a chilly fall day. A girl went to a clinic with her mom. The girl wasn't sick. Instead, she was getting a flu vaccine. It would help her body fight off disease.

**Many vaccines are given as shots.**

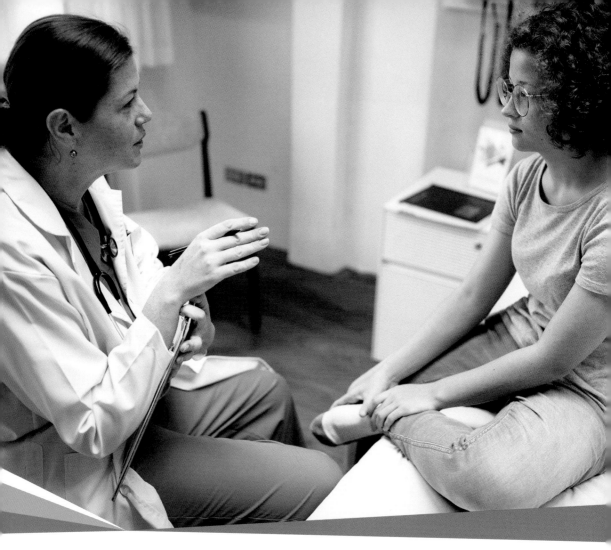

 **Doctors and nurses help people understand what vaccines they should get.**

At the clinic, a nurse asked the girl some questions. He made sure the vaccine was safe for her.

Next, he **disinfected** part of her skin. Then he gave her a shot. He **injected** the vaccine into her arm. The nurse put a bandage over the spot.

That winter, the girl's best friend got the flu. He felt sick for a week. But the girl stayed healthy. The vaccine made her **immune**.

**Did You Know?**

Scientists made the first flu vaccine in 1938.

# Chapter 2

# The History of Vaccines

Vaccines help keep people from getting sick. For example, smallpox used to kill many people. But people in Asia and Africa found a way to prevent the disease. They used bits of smallpox sores.

 **Vaccines helped prevent smallpox from spreading or making people sick.**

They put the bits in people's noses. These people didn't get sick.

In 1796, Dr. Edward Jenner used a similar idea. He made a vaccine for smallpox. Jenner made small cuts on people's arms. Inside, he put parts of cowpox sores. Cowpox is similar to smallpox. But it is

**Did You Know?**

Jenner invented the word *vaccine*. His treatment used cowpox. *Vacca* is a Latin word for "cow."

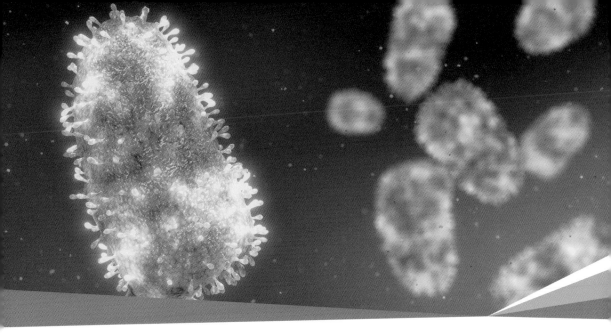

 **Viruses cause some diseases, such as rabies. Bacteria cause others. All these germs are tiny.**

less dangerous. Jenner's vaccine worked. It kept people safe from smallpox. But no one knew why.

In the 1880s, Louis Pasteur proved that **germs** can cause diseases. He used this idea to create several different vaccines.

One was for rabies. Before the vaccine, this disease killed most people who got it.

Understanding germs helped scientists make more vaccines. Some helped stop diseases that spread quickly. Others helped stop diseases that harmed children. For example, polio left many children **paralyzed**. Dr. Jonas Salk studied the **viruses** that caused polio. In the 1950s, he made a vaccine that protected against those viruses.

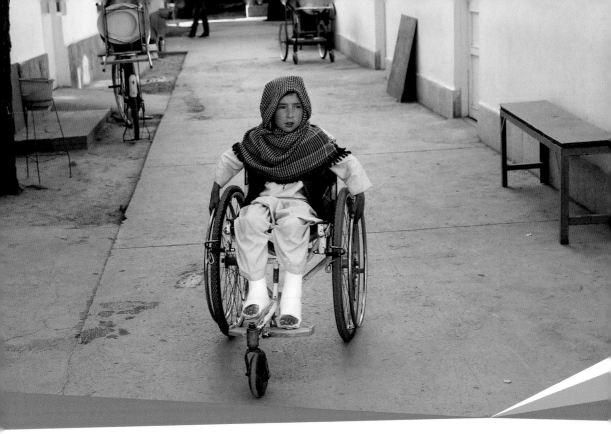

After getting polio, some people can't walk. They need wheelchairs or leg braces.

Vaccines for measles, mumps, and rubella were made in the 1960s. These diseases used to kill many children each year. But thanks to vaccines, they have become rare.

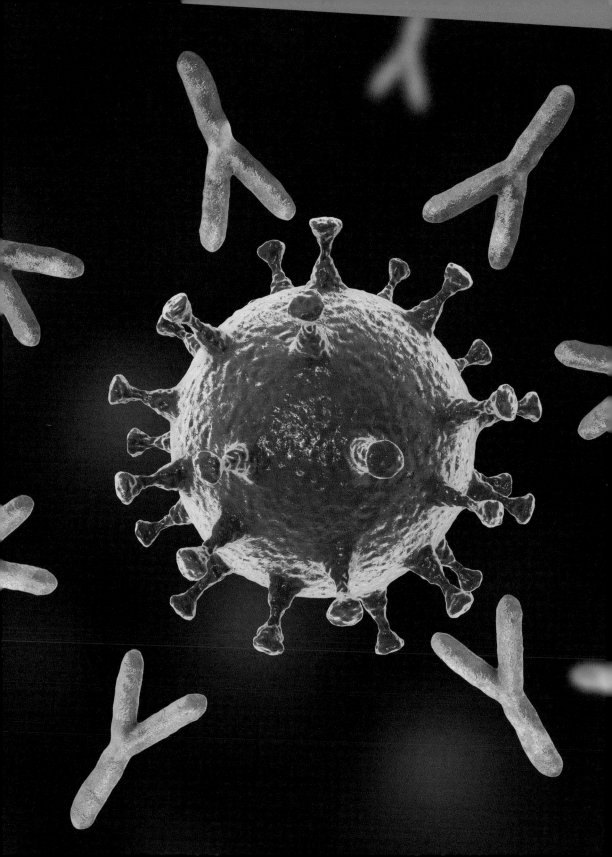

# Chapter 3

# How Vaccines Work

Vaccines help the body fight disease. They work with the **immune system**. This system finds and attacks germs. **Antibodies** help it do this. Each antibody is shaped to match a certain germ.

 **Antibodies look similar to the letter Y. The forked end sticks to germs.**

If that type of germ enters the body, antibodies stick to the germ. They tell the body to attack it.

Vaccines teach the body to make antibodies. These antibodies help the body **identify** certain germs. This helps the immune system fight off those germs. It can kill them

## Did You Know?

Allergies happen when the immune system makes a mistake. It attacks something harmless, such as food.

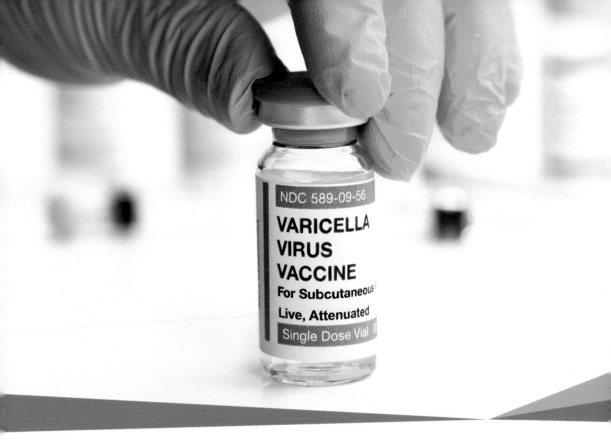

> The vaccine for chicken pox uses a small amount of a live virus.

more quickly and easily. As a result, the person doesn't get sick.

Some vaccines have dead germs in them. Other vaccines use germs that have been made weak.

The body responds to these dead or weak germs. It learns to make antibodies for them. Then the person becomes immune to the disease.

Other vaccines use just part of a germ. Or they use a substance it makes. These vaccines can't cause the disease. But they still teach the body how to fight it.

Many vaccines enter the body as shots. Others are taken by mouth. People may swallow pills or drops.

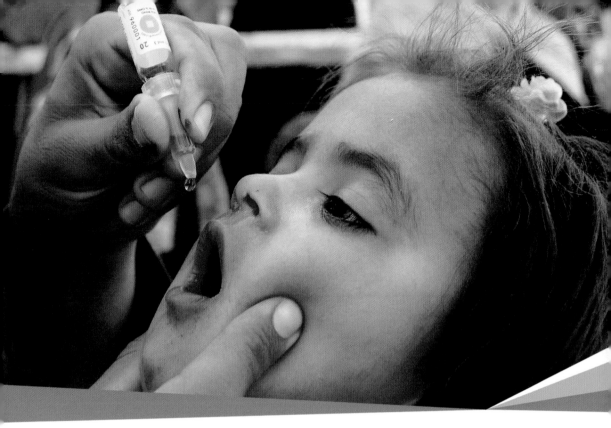

 **One type of polio vaccine uses drops that go in people's mouths.**

People get some vaccines just once.

Then they are protected for life.

Other vaccines don't last as long.

People may need another dose

later on.

# Herd Immunity

Many diseases spread from person to person. Sick people can spread germs to others. Often, those other people get sick, too. However, vaccinated people are much less likely to get sick. They also tend not to spread the disease to others. In fact, they can help stop diseases. When enough people are vaccinated, diseases can't spread as easily. This is called herd immunity.

Herd immunity is important in stopping diseases. It helps keep people safe. Some people can't get vaccines. Some are too old or too young. Others have weak immune systems. Herd immunity can help them not get sick.

# Stopping the Spread

When few people are vaccinated, many people can get sick.

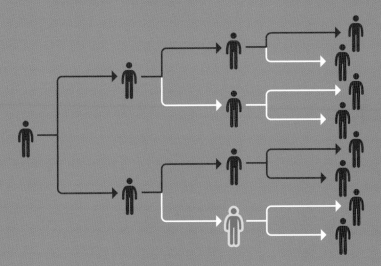

When more people are vaccinated, fewer people get sick.

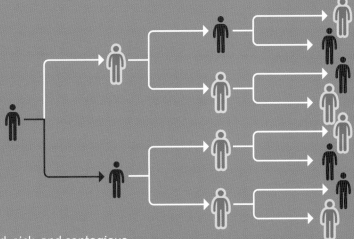

- ● not vaccinated, sick, and contagious
- ○ vaccinated and healthy
- ● not vaccinated but still healthy

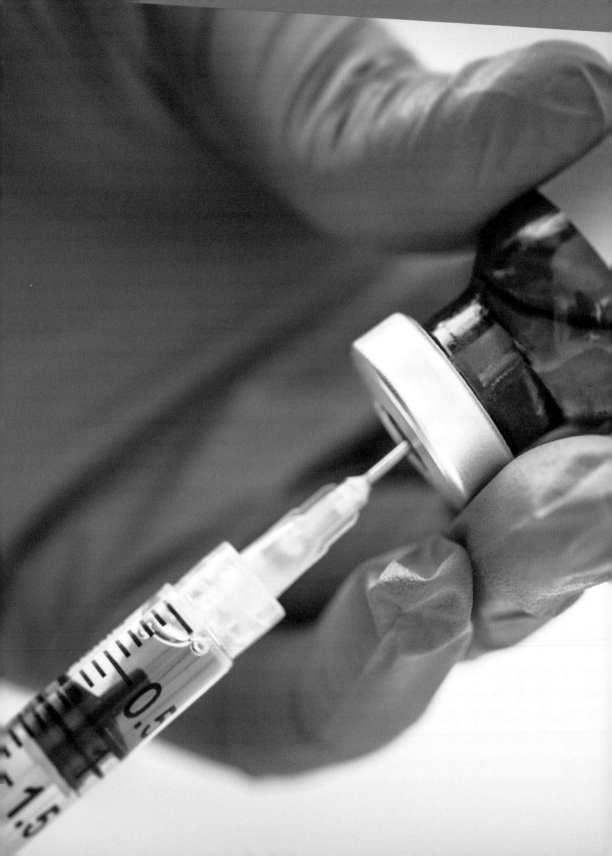

# Chapter 4

# Saving Lives

Because of vaccines, several diseases have become rare. For example, many children used to get polio. Today, many countries have no polio cases.

 **By preventing dangerous diseases, vaccines can save many people's lives.**

Getting vaccines to people can be difficult. Some places are hard to reach. They may not have good roads or ways to travel. Or they may not have workers who can give vaccines.

Plus, some vaccines are expensive. Rich countries can buy

## Did You Know?

Many vaccines must be kept cold. Some places don't have ways to store them safely.

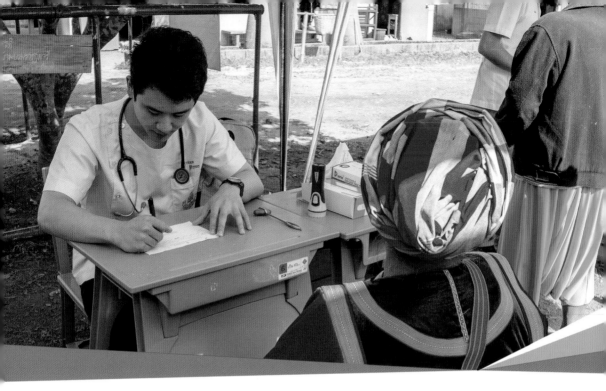

 **Workers at traveling clinics bring health care to hard-to-reach places.**

lots of them. Poorer countries cannot. They often struggle to get enough vaccines. People are working to solve these problems. They try to make vaccines cheaper and easier to get.

 **Some scientists study germs and how they spread. These scientists often work in labs.**

Scientists continue to make new vaccines. In 2020, the COVID-19 virus spread around the world. It killed millions of people. Scientists raced to make vaccines for it. By early 2021, several were available.

Some germs **mutate**. Vaccines may not work against the new germs. For example, there are many versions of the flu virus. So, people get a new flu shot each year. Scientists try to make a vaccine that protects against the versions that are spreading. Their hard work helps people stay healthy and safe.

**Did You Know?**

Sometimes, diseases spread from animals to people.

# FOCUS ON
# Inventing Vaccines

*Write your answers on a separate piece of paper.*

1. Write a paragraph explaining how the immune system fights germs.

2. Would you like to be a scientist who works on new vaccines? Why or why not?

3. Which disease often left children paralyzed?
   A. smallpox
   B. polio
   C. rabies

4. Why can't people with weak immune systems get some vaccines?
   A. Their bodies will heal too quickly.
   B. Their bodies will fight off the germs in those vaccines too easily.
   C. Their bodies might not be able to fight off the germs in those vaccines.

**5.** What does **prevent** mean in this book?

*For example, smallpox used to kill many people. But people in Asia and Africa found a way to **prevent** the disease.*

    **A.** to make something worse

    **B.** to stop or avoid something

    **C.** to win a prize

**6.** What does **rare** mean in this book?

*These diseases used to kill many children each year. But thanks to vaccines, they have become **rare**.*

    **A.** not common

    **B.** more common

    **C.** more fun

*Answer key on page 32.*

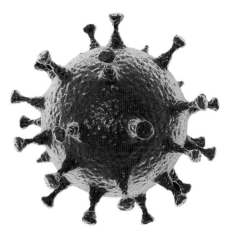

# Glossary

**antibodies**
Proteins that help the body fight infections by attaching themselves to germs.

**disinfected**
Cleaned something to get rid of germs.

**germs**
Tiny things that can cause illness. Germs include viruses and bacteria.

**identify**
To learn or know what something is.

**immune**
Able to resist or fight off a disease.

**immune system**
The body system that fights off infections.

**injected**
Sent something into a person's body.

**mutate**
To develop a new trait as a result of changes to genes.

**paralyzed**
Unable to move a part of the body.

**viruses**
Tiny substances that can cause illness in people and animals.

# To Learn More

## BOOKS

Borgert-Spaniol, Megan. *Your Amazing Immune System*. Minneapolis: Abdo Publishing, 2021.

Goldstein, Margaret J. *The Search for Treatments and a Vaccine*. Minneapolis: Lerner Publications, 2022.

Kaiser, Brianna. *Smallpox: A Vaccine Success*. Minneapolis: Lerner Publications, 2022.

## NOTE TO EDUCATORS

Visit **www.focusreaders.com** to find lesson plans, activities, links, and other resources related to this title.

# Index

**Answer Key: 1.** Answers will vary; **2.** Answers will vary; **3.** B; **4.** C; **5.** B; **6.** A

# TOP TRADE
## CAREERS

# CONSTRUCTION
# MANAGER

**B. Keith Davidson**

Crabtree
Branches